CNSBORO

Eno River
State Park

Falls Lake Res.

RALEIGH

Jordan Lake
Rec. Area

Lake

Uwharrie Nat.
Forest

Raven Rock
State Park

South River

Cape Fear River

Black River

Tar River

Roanoke
River

Merchant Millpond
State Park

Albemarle Sound

Nags Head
Woods

Lake
Phelps

Alligator
River

Cape Hatteras
Nat. Seashore

Lake
Mattamuskeet

Pamlico Sound

White
Oak River

Ocracoke
Island

Core Sound

Cape Lookout
Nat. Seashore

Bogue Banks

Lake
Waccamaw

Onslow Bay

WILMINGTON

Green Swamp

Cape Fear

IMAGES OF WILDNESS

NORTH CAROLINA

PHOTOGRAPHY BY
GEORGE HUMPHRIES
FOREWORD BY DENNY SHAFFER

WESTCLIFFE PUBLISHERS, INC. ENGLEWOOD, COLORADO

ACKNOWLEDGEMENTS

This book would not have been possible without the help, knowledge, support, and encouragement of the many individuals I came in contact with over the three years I worked on this publication. Whether their interest in the well-being of North Carolina is personal or professional, these people all share a love for the land and are earnestly committed to preserving the integrity of our state's rich natural heritage.

I owe the deepest affection and gratitude to my wife, Linda, for her love and support during this undertaking. Thanks to my publisher, John Fielder, a native North Carolinian and master photographer who was willing to take a chance on me. I also wish to thank my best friends: John Tingle, my biggest fan and critic, and Bill Duyck, whom I respectfully call "Dr. Duyck," because of his knowledge of the mountains. Thanks to California friends and photographers Larry and Donna Ulrich, master seers who offered encouragement along the way. I am very grateful to Bob and Gussie Grey for telling me about the turkey beard and cardinal flowers, Jack Dermid for showing me the unique habitats around Boiling Springs Lakes in Brunswick County, and Rodney Rogers for taking me down the Lumber River. I'd also like to thank the following people for allowing me to photograph scenic parts of their property: John Pat Buie (Buie's Pond), Bill Holmes (Laurel Mill), James Lewis (the crab house at Oyster Creek), and Barbara Smith (cypress slough at Moyock). Special thanks to Frank Tipton (Pro Color Lab, Gainesville, Florida) and to Freida Smith for proofing my copy. I would also like to convey my appreciation to rangers Marsha Bowers and Lillian McElrath for their assistance along the Blue Ridge Parkway.

The North Carolina Nature Conservancy: I applaud their tremendous work in preserving the state's threatened ecosystems. I am most grateful to a number of people on the Conservancy staff for their help in providing information about unique habitats in North Carolina and in providing access to Conservancy lands. I would especially like to thank Merrill Lynch for his guidance early on; Ida Phillips, who scheduled me to visit the Conservancy's preserves at Black River and Bluff Mountain; Jeff Smith, who provided access to Nags Head Woods; and Andy Goode for assisting me at Bluff Mountain.

The North Carolina Natural Heritage Program: This unit of the Division of Parks and Recreation was created to identify significant ecological areas in order to protect our state's natural endowment. Special recognition and thanks go to the Heritage staff for their great work in carrying out this mandate. Thanks to Harry La Grande and Steve Hall for helping me with the Piedmont chapter.

North Carolina State Parks: The dedicated men and women who run our state parks are the unsung heroes in the struggle to protect North Carolina's unique habitats. Often working long hours for low pay, they are motivated by their love of the land. Special thanks to Sid Shearin (Pettigrew State Park); Walter Gravley (South Mountain); Tim McCree and David Cook (Morrow Mountain); Tommy Wagner, Jay Zdow, and Tom Jackson (Hanging Rock); Sam Bland (Hammocks Beach); Dennis Helms (Merchant Millpond); Paul Hart (Raven Rock); Susan Tillotson (Eno River); and Jay Sox (Crowder's Mountain).

Finally, I wish to acknowledge the following publications, which I found extremely useful both in the field and in captioning the book: *A Directory to North Carolina's Natural Areas* by Charles E. Roe; *North Carolina Hiking Trails* by Allen de Hart; *Wildflowers of North Carolina* by William Justice and Ritchie Bell; *The Blue Ridge Parkway Guide* by William G. Lord; various articles from *Wildlife in North Carolina*, Jim Dean, editor; and literature on state parks provided by the North Carolina Department of Natural Resources.

International Standard Book Number: 1-56579-042-1
Library of Congress Catalogue Card Number: 93-060056
Copyright: ©1993, George Humphries. All rights reserved.
Photography and captions by George Humphries
Editor: John Fielder
Managing Editor: Suzanne Venino
Creative Director: Leslie L. Gerarden
Printed in Singapore by Tien Wah Press (Pte.), Ltd.
Published By Westcliffe Publishers, Inc.
    2650 South Zuni Street
    Englewood, Colorado 80110

First Frontispiece: Linville Falls in winter, Linville Gorge Wilderness, Burke County

Second Frontispiece: Maples in autumn, West Fork of the Pigeon River, Pisgah National Forest, Haywood County

Third Frontispiece: Old scallop house at dawn, Core Sound, Cateret County

Fourth Frontispiece: Rhododendron frame Graybeard Mountain and the distant Blue Ridge, Yancey County

Opposite: High tide assaults the Cape Hatteras Lighthouse, Cape Hatteras National Seashore

CONTENTS

Above: Beech and maple leaves in a pothole along the South Toe River, Yancey County
Opposite: Duckweed, cypress trees, and tupelo gum in Soules Swamp, Columbus County

FOREWORD

The towheaded boy tossed the bait as far as he could into the marsh, then pulled the string slowly back. The man standing next to him scooped up the crab that followed and dumped it into the pail, the beginning of their evening meal. I was, over 50 years ago, that towhead, visiting the coast of North Carolina with my family.

Chance later led me to business opportunities in North Carolina, so in 1954 my wife, Betty, and I moved here. It was, in fact, a homecoming. Since my first visit to that grand salt marsh, filled with more life than my young mind could have imagined, I have been living out a long love affair with nature.

The natural world—the woods, streams, and fields—was

always an important part of my life growing up in rural Pennsylvania. My dad was a victim of muscular dystrophy but found ways to share with me his great curiosity about the earth and everything on it. Sunday drives took us through the mountains he couldn't hike, taking every unpaved, dusty road he could find. The conversations were of trees and birds. We stopped to examine the flowers growing near the road. It was as if he had read to me the first chapter of a mystery, then given me the book.

My curiosity awakened, I went out. Alone mostly, I walked the mountains, watched groundhogs play, chatted with chipmunks, and sat in cool streams on hot August days observing the crayfish and minnows at play.

Now I was in North Carolina, with its exquisitely complex environment. What did this new "book" contain? I had read about Mount Mitchell, at 6,684 feet, the highest mountain in the eastern United States. And the Uwharrie Mountains, reportedly the oldest in the country; Jockey's Ridge, the tallest sand dune on the East Coast; and one of the oldest rivers—paradoxically called the New—which for some 100 million years has expressed its independence by being our only major river that runs north. And, of course, the Great Smoky Mountains and the Outer Banks.

But time was a scarce commodity in those days, with businesses to run and the birth of two sons. Yet we began to explore. Then, in 1972, my wife died at the age of 42.

The boys and I found in wild places a way to heal. Weekends became times for walks with Sierra Club friends, time to better know each other in the beauty of North Carolina's wild places, walking together in the mountains, on the beaches, and through the hills. The memories are filed in glorious detail. I can see clearly one early morning on the bald of Roan Mountain, the rhododendron in full bloom with their deep purple enhanced by the rosy pink of first light. Cobwebs spun by thousands of unseen spiders hold the night's dew and sparkle like a field of crystals. The air is clean and cool and damp. The memories are many, and they are rich.

Walking the marsh on Masonboro Island on a spring evening, we find a willet on her nest. Bird, nest, eggs, marsh grass...all the same coloration. Then, after sleeping on the beach, we take a morning walk. Unwittingly we near a nesting area of least terns and are driven away by the kamikaze dives at our heads by the tiny birds, determined to protect their own.

Rounding a trail along the river, it is a brisk February day in the Smokies. Then we see it—*our* waterfall. It looks just as we knew it would—half ice, half water. The mist covers everything with ice. Nothing, it seems, can be that white.

Walking through Weymouth Woods we find dwarf irises in bloom. Just five inches tall, they are miniature models of those in our yard at home. Then a pitcher plant with its heavily veined leaves, half filled with water and insects. Now we are on our hands and knees looking for another insect-eating plant—the tiny sundew, just emerging from the moist earth.

It is misty and gray on Pea Island Game Preserve. The migratory birds are like kids at a family reunion. There's a variety of ducks and tens of thousands of Canada and snow geese. Then, suddenly, thousands of whistling swans fly directly overhead, their powerful wings thrusting through the air. The sound? Perhaps like all the dried, fallen leaves in the world, caught in a giant, swirling wind.

It's a bright day as we walk out of Smokemont Campground, and beams of light from the sun pattern the

Above: Sunrise from Daniel's Ridge, above the fog-filled valleys of Transylvania County

ground through the yellow-green leaves of spring. Sam Thomas is leading our search for wildflowers, and they are everywhere. Trilliums, whorled loosestrifes, dutchman's beeches, and several kinds of orchids. There are some 1,400 species of flowering plants in the Smokies. We lose count of how many we find.

There it is—the sign marking the border of the wilderness addition to Joyce Kilmer Memorial Forest. We all worked so hard on this one. The endless phone calls and letters, a trip to Washington to lobby. Now the Eastern Wilderness Bill is law. This special place is protected, forever, as wilderness. Tears are in my eyes as we walk. We do what our opponents accuse us of—we hug a giant tulip poplar. And we hope that Joyce Kilmer looks on.

The photography of George Humphries shows you, better than my words, the land and water and skies of my state. It shows, too, the richness of North Carolina, a richness that has a long history.

In the spring of 1584, two small ships neared what is now the North Carolina coast. Outfitted by Sir Walter Raleigh, they were searching for the New World. Captain Arthur Barlowe, later writing to Raleigh, said, "...we found shoal water, which smelled sweetly, and was so strong a smell, as if we had been in the midst of some delicate garden." George Humphries' photographs reflect the beauty of that garden.

What is the value of natural places? As a businessman, I can talk about their worth as tourist attractions. Over seven billion dollars a year is spent on travel in North Carolina, and scenic beauty and historic interests are the two reasons most given for that travel.

But I am uncomfortable valuing these places in dollars. It's a bit like pricing Michelangelo's David, suggesting that you could get another for that amount. I just know that these places have great value. The world would be much less without them. So would we.

Yet they are there, in many cases, only by the will of the people. Some are protected by law, but we best remember each law was passed over the well-financed opposition of developers. And the developers have their eyes on those places not yet protected.

The struggle continues as the U.S. Forest Service plans for the future management of our national forests. But they often cut too many trees, build too many roads. The Sierra Club and other conservation organizations will save some wilderness, but some will be destroyed.

We have a good Coastal Management Plan, but the last administration did not have the political will to use it wisely, and, consequently, real damage was done. If we do not work together to protect it by law and through sound management, much of North Carolina's natural beauty will be cut, scraped, filled, graded, or paved. "Improved," as the developers say.

Three years ago, my daughter, Francesca, came into my life. I recall the comment of a friend. He smiled as he said, "I wish for every man a daughter." I had no idea what he was talking about then. I do now.

It is not that I love her more than my two sons, now fine men. I couldn't. It is that I love her differently. I'm more protective. I want to hold her close, to keep her safe. My friend knew I would.

So I close with this wish for you. I wish you a few moments alone, or with someone you love, in some of the special places shown in George Humphries' photographs. I wish you to see them first hand, in the ever-changing light. The wish, too, is for you to hear them. Be quiet, and listen. Our modern life trains us not to hear much that is around us, so it will take a bit of effort. Listen closely.

Then smell the clean, moist air, the layers of fragrances unfolding one by one, like the taste of a fine wine. Close your eyes and smell. It is there—"the delicate garden" that Captain Barlowe reported. Knowing these places, seeing, hearing, smelling, touching these places will be, if you permit, a great love.

I know what my friend wished for me. I know you will want to protect these places you love. Sensing their vulnerability, you will want to hold them close, keep them safe, and preserve them for your next visit—and for your children and their children. And, I hope, for this little towheaded daughter of mine.

— DENNY SHAFFER

Former president of the Sierra Club, Denny Shaffer has been actively involved with the organization for more than 15 years. For his statewide work as an environmentalist, he received the 1983 Governor's Award for "the highest designation of appreciation for distinguished meritorious service to the People and the State of North Carolina." A businessman and self-professed "do-gooder," Mr. Shaffer has been described as "the last of the southern evangelical environmentalists."

PREFACE

*Every part of this earth is sacred....Every shining pine needle, every sandy shore,
every mist in the dark woods, every meadow,
every humming insect. All are holy.* — Chief Seattle, 1852

It was a crisp, blue-sky October day as I began hiking the Tanawha Trail. Tanawha is a Cherokee word meaning "fabulous hawk." It is the name they gave to the mountain we call Grandfather. The path I followed cut through a vivid mosaic of fallen leaves. Splashes of color caught my eye at every glance. The pungent aroma of forest decay filled my nostrils. I breathed deep! Just before I reached the footbridge, the refreshing sound of rushing water cascading down the mountain played on my ears. I love the woods in autumn—the sights, the scents, the sounds. Slowly, I made my way up through the oaks, hemlocks, beeches, and hickories. Then, abruptly, the huge trees gave way to gnarled rhododendrons and jagged rock pinnacles. As I crested the first ridge, a magnificent vista opened before me. No wonder early explorers thought that Grandfather Mountain was the highest peak in the East. The drop in elevation from mountaintop to the Piedmont is 4,000 feet, the greatest relief found anywhere along the Blue Ridge escarpment. This extraordinary view inspired Andre Michaux to sing the French national anthem when he scaled Grandfather in the 1790s.

Around me, the steep, forested slopes were ablaze with the yellows and reds of sugar maples, sassafras, and mountain ash, even the golden flicks of aspen leaves shimmered in the breeze. What a strikingly beautiful canvas nature had painted this day—a rich melange of vibrant color interrupted only occasionally by the emerald green of Fraser firs and the lighter greens of trees yet to turn.

For a year I had waited to catch the last light of the autumn sun on the weather sculpted rocks along what is appropriately called Rough Ridge. I set up my camera on a rocky ledge and framed the scene I had waited so long to capture—Hawksbill and Tablerock in the distance with McRae Peak towering above me. Suddenly, I heard the plaintive cry of a raven as it rode the wind currents rising over the mountain. I knew the spirit of the mountain was with me. While I stood there the sun began to sink, illuminating the rocks with a wonderful warm glow. The low angle of its rays stretched the shadows, modeling the contours and defining the textures of the primeval forms beneath my feet. After taking several exposures, I sat there on that ancient rock face intoxicated by the hypnotic effect—ridge giving way to ridge as far as the eye could see. As the sun disappeared below the horizon, the sky exploded in pastels of red and pink. Gradually, these delicate hues faded to twilight. And slowly, almost imperceptibly, stars began to appear. I unrolled my sleeping bag and settled in amidst the rocky crags. The night sky was unusually clear, and the Milky Way, to quote Theodore Roosevelt, was "glorious in my eyes."

For almost three years I had been working to capture on film the special character and scenic wonders of North Carolina for this book. That night as I lay there pondering the mystery of the glimmering spectacle above me, I thought about our extraordinary natural heritage—the beauty, diversity, and vitality of the Eden we call North Carolina. From the narrow ribbon of barrier islands known as the Outer Banks to the Blue Ridge and Great Smoky mountains, North Carolina encompasses the highest coastal dunes, waterfalls, and mountains in the eastern United States. The rivers, cypress swamps, coastal sounds, and the wealth of flora and fauna found here all contribute to the enduring strength and breathtaking beauty of our state.

With its relatively mild climate, abundant rainfall, fertile fields, and magnificent forests, North Carolina is a blessed land, a land made for living in. Its great natural bounty nurtured the state during its infancy and still provides our sustenance today. Through our contact with the land we sustain our identity, our sense of history. But this relationship goes much deeper than cultural and historical considerations. North Carolinians have an emotional attachment to the land—it is the essence of who we are. And whether we realize it or not, we are connected in the most fundamental ways to its primordial rhythms, its cycles of seasonal change, and its unending patterns of life, death, and renewal.

While travelling across the state taking photographs, it became apparent to me that North Carolina is at a crucial juncture environmentally. Wild lands throughout the state are being developed at an accelerated pace. Many biologically significant ecosystems and communities are threatened with extinction, including maritime forests, longleaf pine savannas, mountain bogs, and piedmont prairies. Development, industry, and the utilization of our natural resources can produce more jobs, more revenue, and a higher standard of living. But only through wise use of our natural resources can we sustain healthy economic growth. It is easy to be seduced by the lure of boom and bust dollars, but exploitation for short-term profits will only undermine North Carolina both economically and ecologically. We need to think deeply about the long-term value of the land.

All around us we see signs that things are not right with the environment. Acid rain imperils our high elevation mountain ecosystems. The bleak, skeletal remains of once-luxuriant forests of red spruce and Fraser fir atop Mt. Mitchell and Clingman's Dome are sad testaments to acid rain's devastating impact. Toxic pollution is destroying the productivity of many of our great rivers and estuaries. Marsh grasses that once flourished in Albemarle

Opposite: Last light on the rocky crags of Rough Ridge, Grandfather Mountain

and Pamlico sounds are vanishing. These are but harbingers of things to come if we do not take seriously the impact we have upon the land. The decisions we make and the actions we take right now will determine the quality of life not just for us, but for future generations of North Carolinians.

I have faith in the people of North Carolina. They are the best people I know. And I am optimistic that they will make the right choices. The tremendous work of organizations like the North Carolina Nature Conservancy further bolsters my confidence. The Conservancy has helped purchase, protect, and preserve more than 335,000 acres in North Carolina, including many pristine and irreplaceable ecosystems—such as the Green Swamp, the Roanoke floodplain, Panthertown Valley, and vast areas along the Alligator River.

The rise and fall of waves breaking on the beaches of the Outer Banks, the ebb and flow of tides in Albemarle and Pamlico sounds, herons and egrets fishing the marshes and cypress sloughs, thousands of trumpeter swans wintering on Mattamuskeet, the meander of the Neuse and rush of the Haw, mist rising from the slopes of the Blue Ridge and Great Smoky mountains—all are rhythms in an ancient drama harking back to the dawn of time.

The Black Mountains are over a billion years old, and along the Black River there are cypress trees that were sprouting before the fall of Rome. These natural wonders take us back to our origins. Like the turning of leaves and the blooming of wildflowers, they reassure us of both the continuity and possibilities of life.

When we view the delicate symmetry and intricate beauty of an atamasco lily, or see lightning flash and hear thunder roll across Big Yellow Mountain, we are stirred by the magic, the mystery, and the power of creation.

Whatever we think or believe about how all of this came to be, it is beyond us. Nature has been at work in North Carolina a long time; we cannot improve upon her labors.

Any feeling and thinking person who surveys the great vista from Roan High Ridge, stands beneath the towering tulip poplars in Joyce Kilmer Memorial Forest, or hears the long withdrawing roar of waves breaking across the cape at Hatteras, knows this to be true. The feelings such experiences evoke confirm in the deepest sense that we are part of the web of life and that our destiny is inextricably linked with the well-being of the natural world.

As I lay beneath the sparkling canopy of the night sky, images of the places I had photographed throughout North Carolina flashed through my mind's eye like the shooting stars in the heavens above me. Images of Linville Falls in winter, sunrise over Core Sound, or the fading light of day on Grandfather Mountain—well, turn the pages, they're all here!

— GEORGE HUMPHRIES

This book is dedicated to my mother, Kathryn Powell, and to my father, Ralph Humphries, who loved North Carolina and taught me that nature is a celebration of life.

Opposite: Murray's Mill, Catawba County

APPALACHIAN MOUNTAINS
Alan Weakley

Rising to 6,684 feet, the Southern Appalachian Mountains of North Carolina are the highest in eastern North America. Formed hundreds of millions of years ago by a series of cataclysmic continental collisions, these mountains were once higher and rockier. In the ensuing years, they have been worn down, thrust up anew, jumbled, thrust-faulted atop younger rocks, shot through with magmas of various compositions, and eroded by wind, water, and ice. Like the face of an old mountaineer, the Southern Appalachians have had a long, hard, wearing existence etched into them.

While lacking the elevation and the rugged, barren grandeur of western mountains, the Southern Appalachians' slopes, peaks, and crags show a gentler beauty and harbor a rich diversity of flora and fauna. "Salamander Capital of the World" boasts one local T-shirt, and similar claims could be made for many other groups of animals, as well as for plants. Lichens, mosses, liverworts, ferns, woody plants, flowering shrubs, and trilliums are just a sampling of the more than 300 plant species endemic to these mountains. A similar pattern is true for animals, although the numbers are unclear, since much of the invertebrate fauna remains to be discovered and catalogued. Why are the Appalachians so unique? The reasons involve the diversity of habitats and the ancient history of the region.

The highest peaks and ranges—Grandfather Mountain, Roan High Knob, the Black Mountains, Great Smokies, Plott Balsams, and Great Balsams—are cloaked with dark coniferous forests of red spruce and Fraser fir. One also finds rocky cliffs and grasslands, called balds, which provide hikers and sightseers with commanding views. In 1835, the Reverend Elisha Mitchell wrote that the visitor "will stand with a great ocean of mountains raised into tremendous billows immediately around him." High cliffs harbor remnants of tundra that thrived here 18,000 years ago, when the climate was vastly different. It is at these high elevations that species more common to cooler northern regions are mixed with typically southern species of plants and animals.

A rich diversity of hardwood forests blanket the mountain slopes: yellow and sweet birch, sugar maple ("sugar tree"), red maple, red oak, chestnut oak, white ash, basswood, Fraser magnolia, hemlock, pine, and scores of other species. Rhododendrons often grow in impenetrable thickets known as "laurel hells." Where the rhododendron is sparse, rich cove forests support an amazing variety of herbs. Many of these are remnant species that were once widespread throughout the northern hemisphere, but are now found only in the Southern Appalachians and in the mountains of Japan and China.

The Linville, Toxaway, Horsepasture, Thompson, Chattooga, Whitewater, and Cullasaja rivers have cut narrow gorges along the boundaries of the mountains and the Piedmont, an area abounding in high cliffs and waterfalls. As the region that receives the highest rainfall east of the Pacific Northwest, the Southern Appalachians support a rain forest ecosystem as well as numerous species of ferns and mosses, many normally found in the tropics.

Bogs, among the rarest and most unusual of the mountains' ecological communities, are found scattered throughout the valleys. Peat that has accumulated for thousands of years acts as a sponge, retaining water and fostering a unique assemblage of plants and animals. Orchids abound in these marshy areas, as do insectivorous plants such as sundews, pitcher plants, and bladderworts. Some bogs even provide mountaineers with cranberries for Thanksgiving dinner!

The mountains have long been the most remote, least altered, and least inhabited part of North Carolina. Recent years, however, have brought new roads as well as extensive tourist, retirement, and second-home development. Long-time residents and newcomers alike need to realize that their dreams of the "good life" depend on saving the scenic beauty and biological riches of the Southern Appalachians. If so, the future will bring many a cool, foggy night with Yonahlossee salamanders foraging on moss-covered rocks beneath a canopy of trilliums.

Botanist Alan Weakley is assistant coordinator of the North Carolina Natural Heritage Program. For the past 15 years, he has worked to locate, describe, and protect the state's remaining ecosystems, plants, and animals. Along with Michael Schafale, Mr. Weakley is co-author of Classification of the Natural Communities of North Carolina. *He is a leading authority on the flora of North Carolina.*

Above: Crested dwarf irises, Pisgah National Forest, Buncombe County
Opposite: Linville River, as seen from Wiseman's View, Linville Gorge Wilderness

To hike Big Creek in early spring is to enter an enchanted realm. Every crack and crevice along its course bursts with fresh green life. I am always renewed by this experience, reminded of the words of Saint Bernard: "You will find something more in woods than in books. Trees and stones will teach you that which you can never learn from masters."

It always thrills me to see yellow lady slippers (right) blooming on the mountain slopes in April. These stunning flowers flash like beacons in the russet woodlands, signaling the miracle of renewal. Yellow lady slippers are infrequent to rare in the mountains and various locales in the Piedmont. Unfortunately, some people still dig them up to sell to apothecaries in the Far East or to dealers in the ornamental plant trade.

Beech trees along Big Creek, Great Smoky Mountains National Park

Yellow lady slippers bloom amid last autumn's leaves, Pisgah National Forest, Buncombe County

Nantahala National Forest is North Carolina's largest, encompassing more than 500,000 acres in the southwestern part of the state. A vast, wild land of cascading waterfalls, rushing rivers, and rugged mountains, it was home to Cherokee Indians before the arrival of the white man. The Cherokee gave the land the name Nantahala, which means "land of the noonday sun," because from its deep gorges one can only see the sun's rays at midday. The great Cherokee chief Junaluska was born and buried in Nantahala.

Some of the most beautiful scenes in the mountains of western North Carolina are created by water falling over the erosion-resistant metamorphic rock of the Blue Ridge escarpment. Crabtree Meadow Falls (right), just off the Blue Ridge Parkway, is a splendid example of this.

Weather fronts collide over Nantahala National Forest, creating a mystical sunset, Jackson County

Crabtree Meadow Falls, Yancey County
Overleaf: Rustic barn near Glen Ayre, Mitchell County

The 2,100-mile wilderness path known as the Appalachian Trail begins at Mount Oglethorpe, Georgia, and follows the peaks of the highest mountains north to the rocky summit of Mount Katahdin in Maine. One of the most scenic sections of the entire trail is the ten miles that run along the crest of the Roan Mountain Massif from Roan High Bluff to Doll Flats, including Round Bald, Engine Gap, Jane Bald, and Grassy Ridge Bald. Hiking out across these ridgetops, which rise 4,000 feet above the fertile valleys and farms below, is like being on the roof of the world.

Rocky outcrops of Grassy Ridge and the distant Valley of the Roan, Mitchell County

The Precambrian rock outcrops (opposite) are mottled with a yellow map lichen. Lichens consist of two very different plants, an algae and a fungus. The fungus provides stability and supplies moisture for the algae, and the algae produces food for both plants. This symbiotic relationship may have originated during the Devonian Period, more than 300 million years ago. Lichen eventually breaks down rock, aiding in the formation of soils. Decaying leaves, broken down by bacteria, add vital nutrients to the earth. These beech leaves (above) blanketed the North Fork of the French Broad River during a late autumn rain.

The North Fork of the French Broad River in autumn, Pisgah National Forest, Transylvania County

Rhododendron is latin for rose tree. The Catawba rhododendron can grow to 15 feet in height and live well over 100 years. According to the beliefs of the Catawba Indians, each June the rhododendron blooms red from the blood of warriors killed in three great battles the Catawba fought against other tribes on Grandfather Mountain.

The American chestnut was once the dominant tree of the Appalachian Mountains. Experts estimate that 25 percent of the eastern hardwoods were once chestnut. In the mountains of North Carolina, these great trees were revered for the utility of their wood and the bountiful mast they produced. They were "bread and butter" trees for both people and wildlife. At the turn of the century, a virulent fungus known as "chestnut blight" was introduced here from the Orient, and within 50 years the American chestnut was decimated. Massive, decay-resistant chestnut logs (right) are still found on the forest floor. Even though the blight continues to kill them, chestnut roots still defiantly send up sprouts.

Weathered branches of a rhododendron, the Black Mountains, Yancey County

Hay-scented ferns and chestnut log, Mount Mitchell State Park

Moon rising above Fraser firs and mountain ash, Richland Balsam Mountain, Haywood County

Native Americans have always felt a mystical bond with trees and with all of nature, through which they are connected with the creative power of the universe. For centuries, the Cherokee and other Indians have viewed trees as the "standing people" and humans as the "walking people," believing that "We breathe for each other. We are kin." Modern science supports this ancient wisdom, for today we know that trees consume carbon dioxide while producing life-giving oxygen. Reservoirs of water, trees constantly absorb and release moisture through transpiration, thus helping to maintain the rain cycle. Because their root systems stabilize the soil, trees prevent erosion, especially in mountainous regions and along riverbanks. And as dead logs weather and rot, they generate new soil. Trees also provide shelter and food for many animals, as well as needed resources for humans. As the Indians sensed, life on this planet as we know it would be impossible without trees.

Maiden Hair Falls, Transylvania County

Standing on a mountain peak at dawn, high above the clouds, watching sheets of fog slide down the ridges is a moving experience. It evokes feelings that touch the very essence of being alive. The six highest mountain chains and peaks in North Carolina—the Black Mountains, Great Smokies, Plott Balsams, Balsam Mountains, Roan Massif, and Grandfather Mountain—have been described as "islands in the sky," referring to their ecological uniqueness. Isolated by height and climate, separated from the warmer valleys and each other, they harbor many rare and endemic species.

The Black Mountains (right), which transverse the Blue Ridge, are estimated to be more than a billion years old. A nine-mile-long ridge of the Blacks includes several peaks over 6,000 feet, among them Mount Mitchell, Clingman's Peak, Cattail Peak, Big Tom, and Potato Knob. The Black Mountains derive their name from the emerald green mane of Fraser fir and red spruce that extends along the ridge crests and gives them a dark or black appearance. Potato Knob is steep and rocky, rising abruptly to 6,440 feet. It offers expansive views of the Asheville watershed, Graybeard Mountain, the Pinnacle, the Blue Ridge Parkway, and the Piedmont. This area is a refuge for black bear, as I found out early one morning when I encountered an energetic 500-pound specimen on the trail.

Fog blankets the Blue Ridge Mountains at sunrise, Blue Ridge Parkway, Henderson County

Morning light on Potato Knob, Black Mountains, Buncombe County

Agriculture has been the mainstay of North Carolina economy since the arrival of the first Europeans. Before that Cherokee Indians farmed small plots of land. Throughout our history, from the Coastal Plain to the mountains, North Carolinians have lived close to the land, eking out a living from fertile fields and valleys. Thomas Jefferson called farming "the noblest profession in the world." Today in North Carolina old barns are falling into disrepair and many fields are no longer cultivated. This change in life-style has been called "the passing."

Late afternoon light on a hay barn and the mountain called Winter Star, Yancey County

Catawba Falls is part of a recent 1,000-acre addition to Pisgah National Forest. More than 100 feet high, these extraordinary falls cascade in successive drops down the mountainside. Bounding this rushing torrent of whitewater are towering hemlock trees. Wild grasses, lobelia, water lettuce, and other plants grow on the moss-covered rocks in the midst of the falls, creating a lush hanging garden. At the foot of the falls, mature beech trees grow from among boulders in the middle of the creek. There are few sounds on earth more joyous than the rush of a waterfall.

Catawba Falls, Pisgah National Forest, McDowell County
Overleaf: Autumn colors after a clearing storm, Graveyard Fields, Haywood County

Mount Mitchell, the highest peak east of the Mississippi, rises 6,684 feet above sea level, an elevation that supports a Canadian life-zone environment. To save its virgin Fraser fir forest from logging, Mount Mitchell was purchased in 1915 and became North Carolina's first state park. Encompassing 1,469 acres, the park runs along the ridges of the Black Mountains. Much of its incredible red spruce and Fraser fir forests have been decimated in the last decade by the effects of acid rain and the balsam woolly adelgid, a type of aphid. The bleak skeletons of Fraser firs caught in the glow of a winter sunset stand as foreboding reminders of man's impact on the earth.

Called bracts, the resplendent red leaves (right) of Indian paint brush *(Castilleja coccinea)* are often mistaken for flowers. These plants are semi-parasitic, feeding on the roots of grasses that grow along woodland borders and in moist meadows. A temperate climate, abundant rainfall, and fertile soils have nurtured the remarkably diverse plant life of the Great Smoky Mountains. Some 1,400 species of flowering plants grow along streams, in coves, and on ridges and peaks. And more varieties of trees are found in the Smokies than in all of Europe. This abundance of plant life earned the Great Smoky Mountains the designation of International Biosphere Reserve.

Fraser fir skeletons against an autumn sunset, Mount Mitchell State Park, Yancey County

Indian paint brush and decaying oak limbs, Great Smoky Mountains National Park

Whitewater Falls, Nantahala National Forest, Jackson and Transylvania counties

One of the most spectacular waterfalls in the East was formed as the Whitewater River (left) cut through the Blue Ridge escarpment. Upper Whitewater Falls in North Carolina drops precipitously 411 feet in two steps, while the Lower Falls in South Carolina drops another 400 feet. Constant spray from the falls, coupled with moderate climate, creates a habitat for variety of tropical ferns and mosses. Growing on the steep gorge walls and along the river is an old-growth forest of mixed oaks, red maples, yellow poplars, hickories, white pines, and hemlocks. The Whitewater, Thompson, Toxaway and Horsepasture river gorges encompass some of the most rugged and wild land in the East. They are biological reservoirs harboring many rare, endangered, and disjunct species of plants. If designated as wilderness, these unspoiled lands would remain forever wild.

Pocket of snow atop Grandfather Mountain, Avery County

Isolated boulders on Jane Bald in Mitchell County give testament to an Ice Age climate on the Roan Mountain Massif during the Pleistocene epoch. To stand on these ancient geologic formations in late June and watch the first light of the summer sun creep across the high ridges, setting Catawba rhododendron and flame azalea aglow, is to witness one of the wonders of this world.

Boulders atop Jane Bald, along the Appalachian Trail, Mitchell County

The purple fringed orchid can be found blooming in cool moist woods and wet meadows at high elevations from June through August. Close examination of these orchids, along with a little imagination, reveals that each individual flower resembles a small bird in flight. One of North Carolina's most beautiful orchids, it is, surprisingly, pollinated by moths. Wood ferns belong to the genus *Dryopteris*, which is Greek for "oak fern."

Purple fringed orchid (Habenaria psycodes) *and wood ferns, Pisgah National Forest*

Europeans first learned to smoke tobacco from the Indians, and by the early 1600s smoking had become fashionable throughout England and Europe. Around 1612, John Rofle introduced West Indian tobacco to Jamestown, thus ensuring the economic survival of the struggling colony. By 1619 the desire for fertile bottomlands and new hunting grounds led explorers, traders, and farmers to follow rivers southeast from Virginia into the Chowan River and Albemarle Sound region that would become known as the "Province of Charles," today's North Carolina. The settlers brought tobacco with them and, as in Virginia, it became a staple crop as well as a way of life. From these humble beginnings in the early 17th century, tobacco farming grew into a multi-million dollar industry and a mainstay of North Carolina's economy.

The West Fork of the Pigeon River (right) originates from Bubbling Spring Branch, which begins on the slopes of Mt. Hardy in the Richland Balsam Mountains. The Big East Fork of the Pigeon starts below Black Balsam Knob. The two forks, both pristine mountain streams that support native brook trout, join at Cruso to form the Pigeon River.

Tobacco drying, Little River, Henderson County

Maple and beech leaves along the West Fork of the Pigeon River, Pisgah National Forest

Yellowstone Prong of the East Fork of the Pigeon River, Pisgah National Forest

44

Pink lady slippers (Cypripedium acaule), *Caldwell County*
Overleaf: Fog-shrouded crests of the Blue Ridge Mountains, Jackson County

The headwaters of the East Fork of the Tuckaseegee River originate in Panthertown Valley at the confluence of Panthertown and Greenland creeks, both prime brook trout waters. This portion of the Tuckaseegee is scenic and unspoiled, supporting a wide variety of plant and animal life. Panthertown Valley is characterized by its broad, flat valley floor, flanked by granite cliffs rising several hundred feet. The North Carolina Natural Heritage Program has determined that there are four rare plant communities in the valley, as well as eight species of globally endangered plants.

Headwaters of the Tuckaseegee River, beneath the Rock Bridge, Jackson County

To stand at Engine Gap and watch the wind create visual poetry as it blows through the mountain oat grass on the high balds is to witness the essence of nature. Who can make from scratch a ragwort or a flame azalea? Who has the imagination to sculpt the bizarre rocks seen on Roan High Ridge? Who, in their wildest dreams, could create such a world? Whatever we believe about how it came to be, it is indeed a precious wonder.

Field of ragwort above the Valley of the Roan, as seen from Engine Gap on the Appalachian Trail

White trillium (Trillium erectum) *against American basswood tree, Great Smoky Mountains*

In early April the Great Smoky Mountains herald the arrival of spring. In the damp, verdant woodlands, a tangle of moss-laden logs and emerging ferns, the earth bursts forth with wildflowers—fringed phacelia, spring beauties, hepatica, phlox, and trilliums (left). Towering above these delicate plants stand tulip poplars, silver bells, yellow buckeyes, sweet birches, mountain magnolias, and hickories—forming multiple layers of a lush forest canopy. The diversity of plants found in these hardwood forests is unequalled in the temperate regions of the world.

Since the early explorations of botanists Andre Michaux and Asa Gray, Grandfather Mountain (above) has been famous for its floral diversity. More recently, the North Carolina Natural Heritage Program declared Grandfather Mountain an "ecological site of global significance," for it provides habitat for more globally rare species than any mountain east of the Rockies. Hugh Morton, the owner of Grandfather Mountain, donated a conservation easement to the North Carolina Nature Conservancy, ensuring future protection of this remarkable ecosystem.

Grandfather Mountain framed by beech trees, as seen from McRae Meadows, Avery County

"For those who have seen the Alps or the Rockies, the Appalachians are not likely to stir the heart. They are, rather, a forest upon a high-rolling floor, and in all the continent, in all the world, I believe, there is no such hardwood or deciduous forest as this. All the beauty of the Appalachians is forest beauty....Everywhere the murmur of leaves, the trickling or rushing of water."

— Andre Michaux, *The Journal of Andre Michaux* (1787)

Big Creek after an early spring rain, Great Smoky Mountains National Park

"Here terminates the great vale of Cowe, exhibiting one of the most charming natural mountain landscapes perhaps any-where to be seen; ridges of hills rising grand and sublimely one above and beyond another, some boldly and majestically advancing into the verdant plain, their feet bathed with the silver flood of the Tanase, whilst others far distant, veiled in blue mists, sublimely mounting aloft with yet great majesty, lift up their pompous crests and overlook vast regions."

— William Bartram (1776)

After a clearing storm, Cowee Mountains, Nantahala National Forest, Jackson County

Detail of rock formations on Black Balsam Knob, Pisgah National Forest

54

"There is a pertinent saying in one of the Upanishads. 'When before the beauty of a sunset or a mountain you pause and exclaim, Ah, you are participating in divinity.' Such a moment of participation involves a realization of the wonder and sheer beauty of existence. People living in the world of nature experience such moments everyday. They live in the recognition of something there that is much greater than the human dimension."

— Joseph Campbell, *The Power of Myth*

Crocuses emerge from sycamore leaves in early spring, Transylvania County

"All things belonging to the earth will never change—the leaf, the blade, the flower, the wind that cries and sleeps and wakes again, the trees whose stiff arms clash and tremble in the dark, and the dust of lovers long since buried in the earth—all things proceeding from the earth to the seasons, all things that lapse and change and come again upon the earth—these things will always be the same, for they come from the earth that never changes, they go back into the earth that lasts forever. Only the earth endures, but it endures forever."

—Thomas Wolfe, *You Can't Go Home Again*

Trees frosted with windblown snow, Pisgah National Forest, Caldwell County

Jane Bald, along the Appalachian Trail, Pisgah National Forest, Mitchell County
Overleaf: Blueberry bushes (Vaccinium vacillans) in autumn color, Avery County

Hanging Rock State Park consists of 5,862 acres in the northern Piedmont. The park lies among the Sauratown Mountains, often referred to as "the mountains away from the mountains" because they stand alone in the Piedmont. Hanging Rock is a rugged quartzite outcrop rising some 200 feet above the valley floor. The peak is rimmed with exposed, weather-hewn sheets of rock and great fractured blocks of stone. Other peaks that rim the U-shaped valley of the park are Moore's Knob, House Rock, and the Devil's Chimney.

Rocky crags of Hanging Rock, Hanging Rock State Park, Stokes County

"Time is but the stream I go fishing in. I drink at it; but while I drink I see the sandy bottom and detect how shallow it is. Its thin current slides away, but eternity remains. I would drink deeper; fish the sky, whose bottom is pebbly with stars. I cannot count one. I know not the first letter of the alphabet. I have always been regretting that I was not as wise as the day I was born."

— Henry David Thoreau, *Walden*

The Davidson River, Pisgah National Forest, Transylvania County

Some of the most scenic and inspiring vistas in North Carolina can be found along the portion of the "Mountains-to-Sea Trail" that runs from Tablerock through the Chimneys and out across Shortoff Mountain. Skirting the eastern rim of Linville Gorge Wilderness, the trail offers stupendous views of both the gorge and the Piedmont. Sheer 2,000-foot quartzite cliffs greet the hiker at every turn. At the amphitheater, great walls of rock form precipices that rival any western landscape. The Chimneys, an area of fissures, twisted spires, and serrated overhangs, stand as powerful testimony to the monumental geologic forces that shaped these mountains.

Fissures and quartzite monoliths give way to Tablerock, Linville Gorge Wilderness

The trail that leads down to Lower Cascades crosses dry ridges covered with pines, hickories, and various species of oak. The gradual descent through the forest gives no hint of the sheer precipice that drops into Cascade Creek Gorge or of the rugged beauty of Lower Cascade Falls. The hard, erosion-resistant quartzite cliffs exposed at Lower Cascades are evidence of the tremendous pressure and heat that created Hanging Rock and the rest of the Sauratown Mountains. Amid dense thickets of rhododendron, Carolina and Canadian hemlocks grow along the roughhewn walls of Cascade Creek.

Lower Cascades, Hanging Rock State Park, Stokes County

John Muir, who travelled through the heart of the Southern Appalachians shortly after the Civil War, may have best summed up the value of wilderness when he wrote, "In God's wilderness lies the hope of the world—the great fresh, unredeemed wilderness." The Linville Gorge Wilderness, located in Burke and McDowell counties, is 10,975 acres of some of the roughest, wildest land in North Carolina. Over millennium the Linville River carved a fantastic gorge as its waters plunged 2,000 feet from the crest of the Blue Ridge to the Piedmont. Today one can see magnificent waterfalls, rushing rapids, and great isolated columns of rock rising from the cliffsides. Bounding the steep rims of the gorge are grand vistas and rugged peaks, such as Wiseman's View, Hawksbill, and Tablerock, which soar more than 2,000 feet above the river. No wonder Linville Gorge has been called "the Grand Canyon of the East."

Autumn along the Linville River, Linville Gorge Wilderness, Burke County

Rushing waters of Chestnut Branch, Great Smoky Mountains National Park

PIEDMONT
Charles E. Roe

Even in the most urban region of North Carolina, a surprising number of unaltered or recovered natural areas survive as refuges for native species and their habitats. The Piedmont, located in the central part of the state, has survived three centuries of intensive settlement, farming, and urban development. More than half of the area is abandoned farmland, now in various stages of reforestation through the process of plant succession. The process is slow, beginning with pioneering sedges and shrubs, then advancing to stands of pines which will eventually give way to the hardwood-dominated forests that prevailed over the Piedmont before settlement and cutting.

The scattered, low mountains rising from North Carolina's midlands reminded colonial settlers of the foothills or "piedmont" region of southern Europe. The name Piedmont came to apply to the entire uplands region, bounded on the west by the dramatic escarpment of the Blue Ridge Mountains and on the east by the Atlantic Coastal Plain. Rapids and waterfalls on southeasterly flowing rivers define the "fall zone," where the Piedmont gives way to the Coastal Plain.

The Piedmont's gentle, rolling landscape, interspersed by the floodplains of small rivers and erosion-resistant ridges and summits, masks a dynamic geologic history. The array of ancient rock and soil types were produced by collisions of the earth's crustal plates, volcanic activity, periods of rifts and faulting, submergence and sedimentary accumulations on inland sea bottoms, and intrusions of magma. Several north-south trending basins, now possessing distinctive soils and topography, were formed some 200 millions years ago during Triassic times when the earth's land mass pulled apart. Huge lakes, once up to a mile deep, slowly filled with sediments from the eroding Appalachian Mountains. Today, these basins are filled with shales, mudstone, and conglomerates.

Most of the native upland forests and prairie-like glades have been lost to logging, farming, and urban development. Gone is the once ubiquitous hardwood forest, with giant chestnuts, oaks, beech, and tulip trees. Gone, too, are the majority of bottomland hardwoods that once bordered the region's rivers. Today, only vestiges of the original habitats survive, mostly found along stream floodplains, on steep slopes and rock outcrops, or on "monadnocks," the eroded stumps of ancient mountains.

Forests on the Piedmont's relatively dry uplands are dominated by a mixture of oaks and hickories, with an understory of dogwood, red maple, sourwood, and black gum— all species that are typical of acidic soils. The most distinctive variety of the upland forest is found on the high rocky ridges and summits. This woodland is dominated by an assortment of oaks, hickories, and pines.

On moist, less-exposed slopes— especially in ravines, on lower hillsides, or on steep, north-facing slopes—deeper and better drained soils support a mixed hardwood forest with well-developed subcanopies and diverse shrub and herb layers.

Swamp and alluvial forests were once found along the floodplains of the Piedmont's rivers. Where the bottomland forests have not been destroyed by development, drainage, or dams, species composition is influenced by differences in sediments, subtle elevation changes, and the frequency and duration of flooding. Swamp forests occur in the wettest places and are dominated by flood-tolerant species, including many varieties of oaks, along with American elm, sweet gum, black willow, and swamp cottonwood. Alluvial forests cover the higher elevations of river levees and terraces, and are dominated by a diversity of hardwoods.

Isolated plant communities more typical of the mountains are found on steep, north-facing bluffs. These cooler "micro-climates" survive as relics from the Pleistocene epoch, when glacial advances caused northern and mountain vegetation to shift southward in their ranges.

Altered by man and time, the Piedmont still retains remnants of the ecosystems that once dominated its rolling hillsides and fertile bottomlands—natural communities now small in area but expansive in scenic beauty.

Charles E. Roe is executive director of the Conservation Trust for North Carolina. For 14 years he managed the State of North Carolina's Natural Heritage Program. He is coordinator for the state Audubon Council, consultant to the North Carolina Nature Conservancy, member of the state Nongame and Endangered Wildlife Advisory Committee, representative on the National Land Trusts Advisory Council, and past director for the national Natural Areas Association.

Above: Field of coreopsis (Coreopsis pubescens), Scotland County
Opposite: Looking toward the Piedmont from Hanging Rock, Stokes County
Overleaf: Early morning sun burns off fog along the Eno River, Durham County

Rocky cliffs along the Yadkin River, Boone's Cave State Park, Davidson County

An 80-foot-long rock crevice on the east bank of the Yadkin River (left) is said to have been used by Daniel Boone, hence the name Boone's Cave State Park. Squire Boone, Daniel's father, brought his family to the Yadkin Valley in 1752. For thirteen years Daniel hunted and trapped in the vicinity of the Yadkin River, honing the skills that would serve him well in his exploration and settlement of Kentucky. His role in building the Wilderness Road exemplifies the pioneer spirit, and his exploits as an Indian fighter, trailblazer, and frontiersman are legendary. Once, as he was headed west, someone asked why he was leaving. Boone replied, "Too many people! Too crowded! Too crowded! I want more elbow room!"

James K. Polk, the eleventh president of the United States, was born on November 2, 1795 on a farm near Pineville in Mecklenburg County (above). Under his presidency, the discovery of gold in California set off the Gold Rush, and the country achieved its greatest territorial growth as a result of the Treaty of Guadalupe Hidalgo, in which Mexico ceded to the United States all or parts of present-day Arizona, California, Colorado, Nevada, New Mexico, Utah, and Wyoming.

President James K. Polk's birthplace, Mecklenburg County

Colonies of smooth sumac *(Rhus glara)* grow in open areas, often where the land has been disturbed. Sumacs are vines, shrubs, or small trees of the genus *Rhus*. The poisonous members of the genus include poison ivy *(R. radicans)*, poison oak *(R. toxicodendron)*, and poison sumac *(R. vernix)*, all of which can cause skin irritation in humans. The harmless staghorn sumac *(R. typhina)* and smooth sumac have red fruits that can be made into "sumac lemonade."

Vibrant red sumac leaves, Wilkes County

Dogwood in flower, Morrow Mountain State Park, Stanly County

Sunset along the South Fork of the Catawba River, Lincoln County

The beauty of a sunset (left) is forever a part of nature's rhythms. "One generation passeth away, and another generation cometh, but the earth abideth forever. The sun also riseth and goeth down, and hasteth to his place where he arouse. The wind goeth toward the south, and turneth about unto the north; it whirleth about continually, and the wind returneth again according to his circuits. All the rivers run into the sea; yet the sea is not full; unto the place from whence the rivers come, thither they return again." Ecclesiastes 1:4-7

Raven Rock (above) is a steep quartzite bluff rising 152 feet along the Cape Fear River. The cliff marks the fall line where the ancient erosion-resistant rocks of the Piedmont give way to the softer sediments of the Coastal Plain. About 800 million years ago, a vast sea—its floor consisting of sand and mud—covered the area. Approximately 400 million years ago, immense pressure and heat radically transformed these sediments into schists, quartzes, and gneisses. Time and erosion uncovered Raven Rock, which takes its name from ravens that once roosted there.

Raven Rock, Raven Rock State Park, Harnett County
Overleaf: Cypress trees in autumn, Buie's Pond, Robeson County

The area known as the Piedmont, or the foothills, is the state's most altered region. Most of the Piedmont's indigenous ecosystems are gone, having fallen victim to timbering and farming. The great hardwood forests of giant tulip trees, chestnuts, beeches, hickories, and oaks that once spread their lush canopy over hills and bottomlands are no more. Only tiny, isolated remnants exist, hinting at the vast stands that greeted early settlers. Yet the Piedmont is still a wooded landscape, with pine forests prevailing and slowly giving way to hardwood species. Untended farmland reverts through a gradual succession—from weeds to shrubs, then pines, and back to deciduous hardwood forests.

Tobacco drying in a barn, McDowell County

The warm, brilliant reds of fire cherry and the subtle, cool greens of water lilies compose an oriental-like scene at Badin Lake. The fruits of the fire cherry can be made into jelly, although they are most often eaten by wildlife. Turkeys, raccoons, foxes, owls, deer, and numerous species of songbirds are found in the woods surrounding the lake. Badin Lake is also a popular spot for humans, who hike, boat, and fish here. Largemouth bass, yellow perch, bream, and sunfish thrive in the lake's waters.

Badin Lake, Uwharrie National Forest

The Eno River begins in Orange County and flows eastward through Durham County, snaking through steep woodlands and low meadows. Sycamores, beeches, oaks, and numerous other trees grow along its banks. At intervals throughout its course, the river is studded with exposed volcanic rocks that create small chutes and rapids. In spring the Eno River is idyllic, with fresh green grasses carpeting the meadows, new shoots emerging from the trees, and flowering dogwoods painting the landscape with delicate color.

The Eno River in early spring, Durham County

The seasons are created as the earth tilts on its axis during its yearly rotation around the sun. The first day of summer, around June 21, marks the summer solstice, the longest day of the year in the Northern Hemisphere. As the earth begins to tilt away from the sun, subtle changes in light and temperature occur—the days become shorter and the weather cooler, triggering biochemical changes in plants that produce striking autumn colors.

Maples in autumn hues with a tinge of lingering greens of summer, Catawba County

Evening light reflected in a farm pond, Alamance County

The vibrant sunsets (left) of recent years are linked to the eruptions of Mount Pinatubo in the Philippines, half a world away. These volcanic explosions sent clouds of ash and sulfur dioxide gas miles into the stratosphere. The ash fell to earth, but the sulfur dioxide combined with water to produce sulfuric acid droplets. These droplets scatter light like a prism, reflecting it back to earth and painting brilliant sunsets. Pinatubo's eruptions are the greatest of the 20th century and should create stunning skies for years to come. As John Muir said, "When we try to pick out anything by itself we find it hitches to everything else in the universe."

The Haw River (above) originates in Guilford County, meanders into Rockingham County, then turns southwest, flowing back into Guilford. It then crosses Alamance and Chatham counties before emptying into Lake Jordan. The river is dotted with rock formations and rapids all along its course. When water is low, it is possible to leapfrog across these stone terraces from one bank to another. The Haw is especially beautiful in the fall when the changing leaves of maples, beeches, and sycamores reflect in the glossy, slow-moving water, creating abstracts of color amid outcrops of stone.

Rock-studded riverbed of the Haw River, Chatham County

Moss pink bloom in early spring in the Piedmont. But perhaps one of the most familiar flowers in North Carolina is the dogwood. In late March and early April, beautiful displays of flowering dogwood *(Cornus florida)* weave a bright white tapestry across the deciduous woodlands of the Coastal Plain and the Piedmont. Later in the season, the same spectacle is repeated in the mountains. Tragically, this beloved tree is in peril, threatened by the virulent fungus Discula, also known as dogwood anthracnose, a disease that has decimated dogwood populations. Since the virus appears to be new, plant pathologists have yet to determine the exact cause or even how it spreads, though one study has linked it to acid rain. The flowering dogwood, signature of spring throughout North Carolina and the South, may unfortunately become but a fond memory.

Spring bouquets of moss pink, Richmond County

Appropriately named, the Rocky River begins in Randolph County and flows southeast across most of Chatham County before joining the Deep River, west of Moncure. The Cape Fear shiner, an endangered fish, inhabits the river. The Septima's clubtail, a dragonfly that lives along the riverbanks, is currently a candidate for the endangered species list. The Rocky, along with the Haw River, is polluted by textile and wastewater discharge, as well as by agricultural run-off.

Boulder-strewn course of the Rocky River, Chatham County

COASTAL PLAIN

Lawrence S. Earley

There is no sign to announce that you are in the Coastal Plain, but the evidence is there to see. From the gently rolling hills of the Piedmont, you cross into a region as flat as a piece of shirt cardboard. Rivers that flowed energetically over rocky Piedmont courses suddenly get lazy as they enter the Coastal Plain, meandering through their floodplains in wide loops and leaving swamps behind in abandoned river channels. The Roanoke, the Chowan, the Neuse, and the Cape Fear

are among the brownwater rivers, so-called because of the sediments they pick up on their winding passage through the Piedmont. Before dams and locks corralled their energies, flooding rivers distributed these sediments across the landscape like a rich uncle. These seasonal floods made many landowners jittery, but they made them wealthy, too.

Rivers rising in the Coastal Plain itself have quite a different look to them. The Black River, the Lumber, the Waccamaw—these are blackwater rivers, although "tea-colored" is perhaps a more accurate description. They take their dark color from the tannin in decaying vegetation. Unlike brownwater rivers, blackwater rivers carry so few nutrients that the bald cypress trees along the Black are wimpy specimens, as skinny as a fasting man. Still, a remarkable stand of bald cypress along the Black contains the oldest trees east of the Rocky Mountains, many of them over 1,000 years old and one calculated to be 1,640 years old.

Water is everywhere in the Coastal Plain, gathered in wetlands of extraordinary diversity. It has been estimated that about 95 percent of North Carolina's wetlands occur here, including the Great Dismal Swamp on the boundary of Virginia and North Carolina, the Green Swamp of Columbus and Brunswick counties, and wildlife-rich bottomland swamps that flank twisting rivers. Additionally, the Coastal Plain holds hundreds, if not thousands, of mysterious Carolina bays, all oriented on a northwest-southeast axis with a sandy lip on their southeast rim. Even today their origins continue to stump scientists.

There are freshwater marshes and beaver ponds and the vast, forbidding wetlands choked with evergreen vegetation that the Indians called "pocosin," which translates as "swamp on a hill." Wetlands are generally among the richest wildlife habitats in the state, frequented by many

kinds of mammals and birds, as well as legions of snakes, salamanders, frogs, and alligators.

The upland areas of the Coastal Plain have better drainage and sandy soils, evidence of ancient seas that once migrated back and forth over the landscape. In this sandy earth the longleaf pine tree was once the dominant species, although it could just as easily grow in more fertile, moister soils. Fire was its friend and benefactor, just as fire also contributed to pocosins, Atlantic white cedar swamps, and other Coastal Plain communities. Frequent fires ignited by lightning storms kept the pine forests open, providing the ideal habitat for the fox squirrel and the remarkable red-cockaded woodpecker, the only woodpecker that builds its cavities in live trees. Decades of fire suppression and the loss of mature longleaf pine trees have combined to make the red-cockaded woodpecker an endangered species.

For thousands of years, fire ruled the landscape, giving the edge to fire-resistant species and keeping others in wet pockets. Fire encouraged the longleaf pines, the orchids, the pitcher plants, and other strange and beautiful wildflowers that grow in such profusion in the Coastal Plain savannas.

Fire and water have left their imprints on everything that grows here, a legacy that has made the Coastal Plain one of the most diverse assemblages of plant communities in the Southeast.

Educated at Holy Cross College and the University of North Carolina at Chapel Hill, Lawrence S. Earley has taught at the College of the Virgin Islands, the University of North Carolina, and the University of Tunis in Tunisia. Since 1980, Mr. Earley has been associate editor of Wildlife in North Carolina *magazine, writing on environmental and natural history topics. He has also written for* Audubon, Nature Conservancy, National Parks, *and* Country America *magazines.*

Above: Dawn along the Alligator River, Tyrell County
Opposite: Water plants, Big Swamp River, Robeson County

Forests of live oak once covered large portions of the Coastal Plain and the Outer Banks. One barren stretch of beach on Hatteras Island is still called the Great Woods, more than a hundred years after the last trees were cut down. The natural curve of live oak trunks were ideal for frames of early 19th-century wooden ships. Demand for this prized wood spurred "live oakers" to ravage maritime forests from North Carolina to Louisiana.

Thanks to the efforts of the North Carolina Nature Conservancy, the U.S. Fish and Wildlife Service, and the U.S. Air Force, more than 144,000 acres of swamp forest along the Alligator River (right) are protected. This forest, dominated by white cedar and cypress, has been described as the best example of its type in the mid-Atlantic region. A sprawling labyrinth of pocosins, peat bogs, blackwater creeks, and marshes gives way to the Alligator River. Creeks flowing into the river provide the northernmost habitat of the American alligator.

Ghostly branches of live oaks, Croatan National Forest, Cateret County

Water lilies (Nymphaea odorata), *Alligator Wildlife Refuge, Dare County*
Overleaf: Reflection in Lake Mattamuskeet, Mattamuskeet National Wildlife Refuge

Marsh pink and wiregrass, Little Island Savanna, Green Swamp, Brunswick County

A swamp forest rims the northern shore of Lake Phelps in Pettigrew State Park. It is but a tiny remnant of the great swamp forest that once covered an estimated four-fifths of the Pamlico-Albemarle peninsula. Amid the wood ferns and sprawling tree roots bloom thousands of atamasco lilies (above). These lilies are also found in a few locations in the western part of the state where one mountain town bears their Indian name—Cullowhee.

A national natural landmark, the Green Swamp (opposite) encompasses 15,722 acres in Brunswick County and is the largest Nature Conservancy preserve in North Carolina. Pocosins, longleaf pine savannas, and white cedar swamps are the major ecological communities found here. The proximity of the water table to the ground surface nurtures an incredible diversity of plants. The Conservancy writes that "in the wetter savannas alongside pocosins as many as fifty species of vascular plants can be found growing within one square meter."

Atamasco lilies (Zephyranthes atamasco), *Pettigrew State Park, Washington County*

Tupelo gum trees, Albemarle Sound, Chowan County

The golden glow of sunset across Albemarle Sound belies the stark environmental reality that the Albemarle and Pamlico estuaries are in serious trouble. The disappearance of aquatic grasses that nurture marine life and waterfowl, frequent algae blooms resulting in massive fish kills, and devastating diseases that eat through the bodies of marine animals all point to the declining quality of this vital ecosystem. Strong measures are necessary to preserve the productivity and biological integrity of these estuaries.

Lone cypress in Albemarle Sound, Washington County

Tannins from decaying trees and leaves produce the dark color of blackwater rivers. The appearance of these rivers is deceptive, for in their natural state they are actually very clean; the Black River is said to be the purist river in North Carolina. When water levels are low, the bright white sand of the river bottom accentuates the amber pigmentation of suspended organic matter, giving the water a burnt-orange look, like that of the Big Swamp River (right). Rings around the trunks of trees growing on the banks and in the sloughs along the river mark fluctuating water levels.

Cypress knees, Currituck Sound, Currituck County

Tannin-stained water in the Big Swamp River, Robeson County

The camellia's rose pink flowers and bright yellow stamens create a striking bouquet. Grown throughout the South as an ornamental, the camellia is a semi-tropical shrub or small tree native to Japan and China. It prefers moist, acidic soils and filtered shade. Blooming in early summer throughout the eastern part of the state, it sprinkles the landscape with bright whites, hot pinks, and deep reds.

Camellia petals, Pasquotank County

The neutral water chemistry of Lake Waccamaw is responsible for the unusual variety of aquatic species here. The Waccamaw killifish and silverside are among the species of fish indigenous to the lake. Mollusks exclusive to the lake include the Waccamaw snail, lance, and spiked mussel. The lake covers 9,000 acres and is the headwaters of the Waccamaw River. There is nothing more stirring than watching the predawn light as it slowly begins to reflect in the placid waters of Lake Waccamaw.

Sunrise on sailboats, Lake Waccamaw, Columbus County

Bald cypress trunk, Lake Mattamuskeet National Wildlife Refuge, Hyde County

Mature bald cypress trees (left) are found on the fringes of Lake Mattamuskeet and around the northern shore of Lake Phelps. The wood of this magnificent tree is extremely resistant to decay and is often referred to as "wood everlasting." Proof of its great durability is evidenced in the dugout canoes found beneath the waters of Lake Phelps. Made by Indians living on the lake shores, these cypress canoes are estimated to be some 4,000 years old. The rot-resistant qualities of cypress wood led to the decimation of great stands in North Carolina and other states where the trees were harvested for commercial purposes.

To stand in a cypress slough (above) as the glow of early morning light streams through a foggy mist, to see a great blue heron fishing in the marsh, or to watch ducks skim the top of the water as they land is to witness the timeless drama of nature. Who among us can deny the wonder, the mystery, the feeling that such an experience evokes?

Sunrise over a fog-veiled cypress slough, near Moyock, Currituck County
Overleaf: Daybreak on the Pungo River, Beaufort County

Merchant Millpond State Park comprises 2,700 acres in Gates County. Its unique blend of coastal pond and southern swamp forest forms one of North Carolina's rarest ecosystems. Bald cypress and tupelo gum trees draped in luxuriant growths of Spanish moss and resurrection ferns dominate the 760-acre millpond, a scene that conjures up images of legendary swamps of the Deep South. Great mats of water lilies interlaced with a variety of other aquatic plants carpet the open blackwater of Merchant Millpond. Rising out of this spectacular mosaic of vegetation are the swollen buttresses of tupelo gum and cypress trees. Further up Bennetts Creek in Lassiter Swamp, old-growth bald cypress grow 120 feet high and eight feet in diameter. Here is the eerie "enchanted forest" of tupelo gum with trunks and branches distorted into fantastic shapes by parasitic mistletoe. A.B. Coleman, a colorful man who loved North Carolina's swamps, gave 919 acres—including Merchant Millpond—to the state with the stipulation that a park be created. When asked why he gave away such a valuable piece of land, he replied that "the millpond was too pretty to be developed and thus destroyed."

Water lilies with cypress trees, Merchant Millpond State Park, Gates County

Marsh with cattails, Tull's Creek, Currituck County

OUTER BANKS
Jan DeBlieu

I first came to the Outer Banks because of the light—sunshine pouring through humid air, reflected back on itself by ocean and sound. Beneath such thick, honey-colored rays the world felt purer, and the spread of land and water seemed to hum with a soft vibrance. But while the beauty of the scenery drew me here, the tenacity of the natives made me want to settle down and stay.

To live on the Outer Banks means sustaining oneself against a constant battering of

salt, wind, sand, and sun. This thin arc of land, stretching for 175 miles off the northeastern North Carolina coast, forms the front line of battle against a moody sea. Geologically speaking, the banks are out on a limb—a string of barrier islands that curl unusually far east, coming within 30 miles of the Continental Shelf. As a result, storm surf churned up by easterly winds hits the shelf and rumbles headlong onto the beaches. The breeze, too, whips across the flat landscape unchecked by mountains or hills. Together wind and surf pummel these ill-placed threads of land, biting at them with erosion and pushing them west in an incremental but ceaseless migration.

Residents here, be they human, animal, or plant, must harden themselves to the elements or find a specialized niche to fill. Despite a recent surge in development, the Outer Banks are still relatively unpeopled, partly because of their notoriously stormy surf and partly because more than half their length has been preserved as the Cape Hatteras and Cape Lookout national seashores. The parks, with their empty coastlines, make ideal places to study how plants adapt to maritime conditions. Only wiry grasses like sea oats crest the frontal dune; they survive occasional dousings of salt water and cling to windblown sand with creeping roots known as rhizomes. A bit west, in the slightly more sheltered dune fields, waxmyrtle bushes, yaupon trees, red cedars, and live oaks hold fast with web-like roots. All have foliage that resists losing moisture, one of the most precious commodities on a barrier island. Their limbs are so pliable they can be shaken like rag mops by the wind.

At their most slender points the Outer Banks are only a half mile across, scarcely more than a sand bar colonized by a few volunteer grasses and shrubs. In a few places, though, they widen to as much as four miles, and

their terrain becomes one of plunging hollows and steep sand ridges. Over hundreds of years these areas have given rise to diverse maritime forests, including Nags Head Woods on Bodie Island and Buxton Woods at the crook of Hatteras Island. Salt-tolerant trees such as live oak and loblolly pine form an umbrella of branches, beneath which grow dogwood, sweet gum, red maple, and other species normally confined to inland forests. Until fifty years ago these woods were homesteaded by islanders who thought it unwise to build on the perilous ocean shore. Now most residents of the Outer Banks prefer to take their chances living on the beach. While the forests have begun to feel the pinch of development, they are still populated by gray foxes, raccoons, deer, snakes, and songbirds.

On the western bank a marsh of cordgrass and needle rush drops into Albemarle and Pamlico sounds. Water exerts a pull upon the land, and land upon the water. Currents and wind-driven tides swirl through inlets and channels, bringing plankton, nutrients, and marine animals from afar. Tropical fish, pushed north by the Gulf Stream, school up around posts and crab pots. Northern species of trout and mullet, carried south on a tongue of the cold Labrador Current, feed in deep sloughs. Crabs and clams burrow into the muck of the sounds, hiding from platoons of long-legged waders: herons, egrets, avocets, stilts.

The banks are cauldrons of life, mixing northern with southern and aquatic with terrestrial. They are the last thin edge of a continent, an oasis at sea for the stout of heart to call home.

Jan DeBlieu is the author of Hatteras Journal, *a book about the natural and human ecology of the Outer Banks. Her second book,* Meant to be Wild: The Struggle to Save Endangered Species through Captive Breeding, *was selected by* Library Journal *in 1991 as one of the three top natural history books of the year. Ms. DeBlieu has written on natural history topics for more than a decade, with articles appearing in such diverse national publications as* The New York Times Magazine *and* Orion, *a quarterly journal of nature writing. Ms. DeBlieu lives on the Outer Banks with her husband and son.*

Above: Morning glories (Ipomoea sagittata) *and driftwood, Cape Hatteras National Seashore*
Opposite: Sunrise over the Atlantic, as seen from Bodie Island
Overleaf: Morning light breaks through clouds over the Atlantic, Cape Hatteras National Seashore

Maritime forests grow on the leeward side of barrier islands, somewhat removed from the intense shearing effect of the ocean's salt spray. Live oak trees dominate these forests, their great sprawling limbs and leathery leaves forming a thick canopy. Sculpted by salty winds and buffeted by gales and hurricanes, the perimeters of maritime forests are shaped into dense, almost impenetrable hedges that protect interior plants and trees from the devastating effects of ocean spray. Inside this deceptive barrier, the forest opens up to an inner sanctuary. Indians once hunted here, stalking deer, wild turkey, and other game that feasted on the acorns that fell from live oaks.

With only 12,000 acres of maritime forest remaining in North Carolina—and much of that threatened—the North Carolina Division of Coastal Management recently declared that "the maritime forest ecosystem is virtually gone in North Carolina." Nags Head Woods (right), maintained by the North Carolina Nature Conservancy, is a 680-acre preserve located in Dare County. It is a superb example of ancient dunes, maritime forest, freshwater ponds, and pine hammocks. Many freshwater ponds are found among the forested dunes, supporting bladderworts and a variety of aquatic plants.

Maritime forest of live oak trees, Ocracoke Island, Cape Hatteras National Seashore

Bladderworts on a freshwater pond, Nags Head Woods, a Nature Conservancy preserve

The sun sets over tidal flats at South Point, Ocracoke Island, Cape Hatteras National Seashore

On the shores of Silver Lake, the quaint fishing village of Ocracoke offers a romantic glimpse of the traditional seafaring way of life on the North Carolina coast. Natives of Ocracoke Island still put to sea in their skiffs and shrimp boats, and even today, more than 300 years after English immigrants settled here, you can hear the poetic sound of the King's English. Ocracoke retains much of its early charm and character, but like the other fishing villages in North Carolina, it is changing as it succumbs to the pressures of tourism and development.

Shrimp boats on Silver Lake, Ocracoke Island, Hyde County
Overleaf: Dawn breaks across Core Sound, Cateret County

The freshwater marsh that inundates the low swales of Buxton Woods is especially beautiful in September, for that is when the dense growth of cattails, grasses, marsh sedges, red maples, ironwoods, dogwoods, and numerous other trees and plants display their autumn color. Migrating birds chatter in the woods and coreopsis bloom profusely throughout the marshes, a last burst of yellow signaling the denouement of the season.

Yellow coreopsis and reeds, Buxton Woods Marsh, Cape Hatteras National Seashore

The ancestors of James Paul Lewis left Portsmouth Village on the Core Banks in 1725 and settled at Oyster Bay. Mr. Lewis, who runs a crab processing house along Oyster Creek, where the Miss Lue is docked, speaks with both pride and a sense of sadness about the vanishing seafaring tradition of his family. The oysters that gave the creek its name were killed off by the early 1960s, victims of agricultural run-off.

The Miss Lue and an old crab house, Oyster Creek, Cateret County

On the northern boundary of Nags Heads Woods, the ancient dunes of Run Hill offer a grand panorama of fresh- and salt-water marshes that extend all the way to Roanoke Sound. Drainage from the forested dunes of Nags Head Woods supports a variety of freshwater plants. To the west is a vast brackish marsh punctuated by small islands called "hammocks" that rise above growths of black needlerush. This rich habitat, constantly being redefined, teems with wildlife.

Built in 1871, the Bodie Island Lighthouse (right) rises 161 feet above the surrounding marsh and maritime forest, dominating the island. The climate of Bodie Island and the rest of the Outer Banks is moderated by the convergence of the warm coastal Gulf Stream current with the cooler waters of the North Atlantic. This climate zone supports a unique mingling of northern and southern species.

Windblown dunes, Nags Head Woods, a Nature Conservancy preserve, Dare County

*Bodie Island Lighthouse in morning light, Bodie Island, Cape Hatteras National Seashore
Overleaf: The day ends over Croatan Sound, Dare County*

A waning moon over the wind-sculpted dunes of Jockey's Ridge State Park

Buxton Woods on Hatteras Island is the largest maritime forest still remaining on the Outer Banks. It is a bizarre tangle of live oaks, red cedar, loblolly pine, and other salt-tolerant species. Moderate climate and steep dunes contribute to this peculiar ecological habitat. In autumn, Buxton Woods hums with the activity of migrating birds stopping over on their journeys south. Filled with plant and animal life, the woods supports a significant population of cottonmouth water moccasins in its marshes.

Water oaks, Buxton Woods, Cape Hatteras National Seashore

The lighthouse on Ocracoke Island is the oldest still in service in North Carolina. The whitewashed brick-and-mortar tower stands 65 feet high and can be seen from any point around Silver Lake. Built in 1823 to help seamen navigate Ocracoke Inlet, the lighthouse has an 8,000-candle-power light that is visible 14 miles out to sea. Unfortunately, Sir Walter Raleigh's colonists had no such beacon to guide them ashore when they landed on Ocracoke in 1585.

Live oaks beneath the Ocracoke Lighthouse, Ocracoke Island, Hyde County

Perhaps the most recognized structure in all of North Carolina is the Cape Hatteras Lighthouse. Built in 1870 and towering 208 feet high, this sentinel beams a welcomed light to mariners sailing the treacherous waters off Diamond Shoals. The shoals are constantly changing sandbars that jut out into the Atlantic from Cape Hatteras. Since colonial times hundreds of ships have sunk in these perilous waters, more than justifying the shoals' gloomy epithet, "Graveyard of the Atlantic."

Cape Hatteras Lighthouse, Cape Hatteras National Seashore
Overleaf: Sea oats and the Cape Hatteras Lighthouse, Cape Hatteras National Seashore

George Humphries made the images in this book using a 4x5 Linhof Master Technika camera, fitted with Schneider and Nikkor lenses ranging from 75mm to 500mm. Shutter speeds varied between 1/60th of a second and 30 seconds, with lens apertures from f/5.6 to f/64. Fujichrome 50 Velvia sheet film was used exclusively. Warming filters (81B and 10 Red CC) were used on overcast days, in shade, and at dusk, and a polarizing filter was used to reduce glare and maintain color saturation.

Sunrise over Bogue Sound, Cateret County

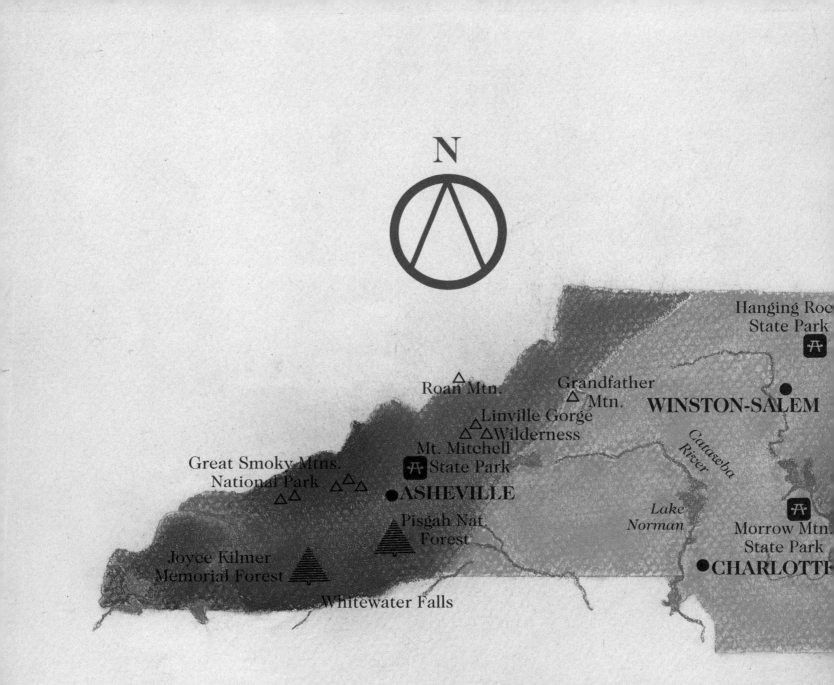

N

Hanging Roc
State Park

Roan Mtn.

Grandfather
Mtn.

WINSTON-SALEM

Linville Gorge
Wilderness

Mt. Mitchell
State Park

Great Smoky Mtns.
National Park

Catawba
River

•ASHEVILLE

Lake
Norman

Pisgah Nat.
Forest

Morrow Mtn.
State Park

Joyce Kilmer
Memorial Forest

•CHARLOTT

Whitewater Falls

NORTH CAROLINA

MOUNTAINS

PIEDMONT

COASTAL PLAIN

OUTER BANKS